# WHY DID GRANDMA HAVE TO DIE?

Kristen D. Randle
Illustrated by Shauna Mooney

Bookcraft
Salt Lake City, Utah

ISBN 0-88494-621-5

First Printing, 1987

Printed in the United States of America

I can hardly wait for Friday night," Christy said. She did a little dance and fell down onto the grass next to James.

"Why? What's going to happen?" James asked.

"Don't you *remember*? We're going to sleep over at *Grandma's*," Christy said, staring at her brother.

"*This* Friday night?" James asked. "I thought we had to wait longer than *that*."

"Nope," Christy crowed. "And I can't *wait!*"

Christy and James loved their grandma. Grandma lived all alone in a wonderful white house, and sometimes the children got to sleep over there in Aunt Gill's old bedroom upstairs. That house was just *full* of old treasures, and Christy and James loved for Grandma to talk about them.

Grandma didn't sew or knit or do very much, but sometimes she made chocolate chip cookies with the children. And when they all worked in the kitchen together, Grandma told stories about how the world had been when she herself was little.

But the best thing about Grandma was the love she had for James and Christy. It was a very special love. Sometimes Grandma put her arms around them, and sometimes she didn't—sometimes she would tell them she loved them, and sometimes she didn't say anything at all. But the children knew—everything Grandma did meant love.

"Now I can't wait, either," James said, and he ran very fast around the yard to show how excited he was.

Later, Christy and James went inside to ask Mother for a cool drink. The moment they stepped into the kitchen, everything began to feel very strange.

Mother was sitting at the kitchen table with her face in her hands, and she was crying.

James felt frightened. When Mother cried, something had to be wrong.

Christy gently put her hand on her mother's head. "What's wrong, Mama?" she asked. Christy began to feel scared and unhappy inside.

James was uncomfortable, and that made him feel angry. Mother opened her arms for Christy, but she didn't say what was wrong.

They heard Daddy's car pull into the driveway. It was usually such a wonderful thing when Daddy got home, but this was not the right time for him to be coming, and it made James feel even more strange and uncomfortable.

When Daddy came in the door, he looked worried. He put his arms around Christy and her mother. Christy began to cry, but she didn't understand why she was crying. James stood there watching, feeling angrier and more upset every minute.

Mother picked Christy up and Daddy put his hand on James's shoulder. They all went into the living room together. Mother sat down on the couch and took Christy onto her lap. Daddy sat down on a chair and put his arm around James.

"Children," he said very gently. "Your grandma died today. She was very old, and her heart stopped working, so her whole body had to stop working. And when that happened her spirit couldn't stay in her body anymore, so her spirit went to paradise, where the good and happy spirits live after this life."

Christy and James didn't really understand at first. "Are we still going to sleep at Grandma's house Friday night?" Christy asked.

"No, Honey," Daddy said.

"Well, can we go see her when she gets back?" Christy asked.

Daddy looked sad. "Grandma's not going to come back, Christy," he said. "She's gone. She's not coming back."

Christy couldn't understand at all. She had to think about it, and think about it. And when she finally did begin to realize that Grandma would never be in her old house again, Christy began to feel sad, sadder than she had ever felt in her whole life.

James was angry. He didn't want anyone to touch him. He pulled away from Daddy and stood with his back to the wall. He crossed his arms and he stared hard at the floor.

"Why did she go?" James demanded. And Christy wondered that, too.

Daddy looked at James for a minute. "James," he said. "Look at your body. Right now you have a good healthy body that can do just about anything you want it to. You can run and jump and play, and you hardly ever get tired. But sometimes bodies get sick, and sometimes bodies get tired and worn out. A body is kind of like a car, James. No matter how much you love it, if there's an accident, and the car gets hurt enough, it can't work anymore. And if the car never has an accident, someday it will just get too old and worn out to run anymore."

"Grandma isn't a car," James said angrily. "She's a *person*."

Mother still had tears on her face, but now she began to talk to the children, too. "You have to understand—Grandma's *spirit* is the *person* part of her. Grandma's body was kind of like a car for her spirit," she said. "Her spirit was like the *person* inside, driving. And her spirit is still alive, even though her body won't work anymore. Grandma is still Grandma. But without her body, her spirit can't make cookies with you or take care of you or hug you the way Grandma used to do when her body worked. Now she has gone to the world of spirits, where she will find out what Heavenly Father wants her to do from now on."

"I want her to be *here*," James said. He was still feeling angry and very stubborn.

"So do I," said Christy. She wasn't angry, but she had an unhappy feeling inside, and she put her head into her mother's lap and began to cry.

"We all do," Mother said, patting Christy's head. "She was *my* mama, and I already miss her very much. But listen, children. Do you remember all those stories Grandma used to tell you about when she was little? Remember the friends she told you about? Remember how much Grandma loved her own mama?

"Where do you think those friends are now, most of them? Where's Grandma's mama? And where's Grandpa? All those people Grandma loved so much were all waiting for her. Grandma stayed with us instead of going to be with them, and she stayed for a long time. Do you think it would be fair, Christy and James, for us to keep her here longer when Grandpa has been waiting for her for such a long time?"

"She's *my* grandma," James said, holding his arms very tight.

"James," Daddy said, "Do you want Grandma to be sick? Do you want Grandma to have to sit in a chair all day and not be able to move or laugh or run like you can? Do you want her always to be old?"

"No," cried James.

"Then you have to let her go," Daddy said gently. "You just have to let her go to where she will be young and happy again. Do you think she could feel happy leaving here if she knew that we were mad at her? Do you think she can be happy right now if her own James is *mad* at her?"

"I'm not mad at her," James cried. "I'm not *mad*." And then James began to cry. He cried very hard, so hard that he didn't even feel it when Daddy came close and held onto him tightly. But that was all right, because crying is what people sometimes have to do when they feel very sad.

After a while, James rested. "She didn't even say good-by," he said. "Why didn't she say good-by to us? I thought Grandma loved me."

"She does, James," Daddy said. "She didn't know she was going away. It just happened. It was a surprise to her. But she still loves you, and now she will be waiting for you, just the way Grandpa was waiting for her. See? You'll see her again when you get there. It's all right to be sad. It's okay to miss her, but we are going to have to face the fact that our Grandma is gone now. She *is* gone. But she's okay.

She's with all her old friends and her family, and best of all, with Grandpa; and though she'll miss us she's probably so happy she can't stand it. It's just hard for us because we're going to miss her and there's no one to take her place. And we're probably going to feel strange inside and want to cry for a while. But that's okay."

"I want to say good-by," James said.

"That's all right," Mother said. "Why don't you do it?"

So James closed his eyes tight, and he said, "Good-by, Grandma. I love you. And I wish you were still here."

And then Christy said, "I want to pray."

"That's a good idea," Mama said. So they all got down on their knees and Christy folded her arms and bowed her head. "Dear Heavenly Father," she said. "Our Grandma has left us and gone to live in paradise. Please take good care of her and make sure she finds Grandpa, and tell her that we love her."

Christy opened her eyes. "I feel better," she said. And she did, even though she still didn't feel very happy.

"Now, there's one more thing," Daddy said. "We're going to have a special church meeting in a couple of days. It's going to be all about Grandma. Your cousins will come, and their families, and we'll all talk about Grandma, and what we loved about her. We'll probably all cry some more and feel sad again because we all are missing her together.

"Her empty body will be at that meeting. It may not be easy to look at her body without wanting her to open her eyes and smile. But just remember, that body was only a part of Grandma, a part she can't use anymore for a while. But the best part of Grandma, the part that made her smile—the part of her that loved you, Grandma, her real *self*—that part is just fine, and she still loves us and she'll be waiting for us, because someday we'll go there too. Do you think you can remember that?"

"I'll try," Christy said.

But James was beginning to worry. "Are you and Mother going to leave, too?" he asked.

Daddy looked thoughtful. "Someday we will. Just like someday you will. Nobody knows when they're going to die. We don't *want* to leave here just yet. So, I'll tell you what—we'll just be as careful as we can. We'll take good care of ourselves, eat good foods, wear our seatbelts when we're in the car, remember our safety rules, and that's the best we can do. Everybody dies, James and Christy. It's part of Heavenly Father's plan.

"But you know, there's another part to this story. You remember what you learned at Easter time? About how Jesus was crucified, but then he came alive again? That is, he was resurrected."

The children could remember that story.

Now Daddy was excited. "That's going to happen to everybody," he said. "When the time is right—and Heavenly Father is the one who decides about that—when the time is right, every person who ever died will get his or her body back—the spirits put right back into the bodies, this time forever. And all the bodies will be just like new, all young and strong and beautiful. And if we all have obeyed Heavenly Father's commandments, we'll be able to stay together. We'll be able to run around and whistle and hug each other again, and we'll just live together with our families, and never worry about dying again."

"Like a family reunion?" Christy said, thinking about how much fun that could be.

Mother laughed. "*Better* than a family reunion," she said, and she hugged Christy. "Want to make some cookies?" she asked.

"*Yeah*," the children said together. "You too, Daddy," James said, taking his father's hand.

"If we do that, it will be almost like going to Grandma's," Christy said happily, "if you tell us some stories while we make them. And then we can eat all the cookies hot with milk." Christy felt better. "It will be like Grandma's going-away party."

Mother laughed again and smiled at Daddy. "It'll be just like that," she said.

And that's just what they did.